ASTRONOMY:
Black Holes, Discovery, And How They sound.

Mark M. Breen

Table Of Contents

How Do Black Holes Sound?

CHAPTER 1

HISTORY AND DISCOVERY OF BLACK HOLES

Black holes are among the oddest and most interesting things in the universe. They are extraordinarily dense, having so powerful gravitational pull that not even light can escape their grip.
The Milky Way might contain around 100 million black holes, yet locating these gluttonous animals is quite difficult. At the center of the Milky Way sits a supermassive black hole – Sagittarius A*.

The massive object is nearly 4 million times the mass of the sun and resides around 26,000 light-years distant from

Earth, according to a statement from NASA.

The first photograph of a black hole was acquired in 2019 by the Event Horizon Telescope (EHT) team. The spectacular snapshot of the black hole at the heart of the M87 galaxy 55 million light-years from Earth wowed astronomers across the globe.

Black Hole Discovery.

Albert Einstein initially predicted the existence of black holes in 1916, with his general theory of relativity. The phrase "black hole" was invented several years later in 1967 by American astronomer John Wheeler. After decades of black holes being recognized solely as theoretical things.

The first black hole ever detected was Cygnus X-1, situated inside the Milky Way in the constellation of Cygnus, the Swan. Astronomers noticed the first traces of the black hole in 1964 when a sounding rocket identified astronomical sources of X-rays according to NASA.

In 1971, scientists established that the X-rays were emanating from a brilliant blue star circling a mysterious black object. It was believed that the discovered X-rays were a consequence of stellar material being stripped away from the brilliant star and "gobbled" devoured by the dark object – an all-consuming black hole.

HOW MANY BLACK HOLES ARE THERE?

According to the Space Telescope Science Institute(opens in new tab) (STScI), roughly one out of every thousand stars is big enough to form a black hole. Since the Milky Way includes about 100 billion stats, our galaxy must host approximately 100 million black holes.

Though identifying black holes is a challenging operation and estimates from NASA predict there might be as many as 10 million to billion-star black holes in the Milky Way.

The nearest black hole to Earth is called "The Unicorn" and is positioned roughly 1,500 light-years distant. The moniker has a twofold meaning. Not only does the black hole candidate lie in the constellation Monoceros ("the unicorn"), its extraordinarily low mass — around three times that of the sun — makes it practically one of a kind.

Black Hole Images

Orange light ring enclosing a black circle.

The Event Horizon Telescope, a planet-scale array of eight ground-based radio telescopes constructed through worldwide cooperation, took this picture of the supermassive black hole in the heart of the galaxy M87 and its shadow.

In 2019 the Event Horizon Telescope (EHT) team revealed the first picture ever captured of a black hole. The EHT spotted the black hole at the heart of galaxy M87 when the telescope was probing the event horizon or the region beyond which nothing can escape from a black hole. The figure depicts the abrupt loss of photons (particles of light) (particles of light). It also opens up a whole new avenue of study in black holes, given that scientists know what a black hole looks like.

In 2021, scientists presented a fresh perspective of the huge black hole at the heart of M87, illustrating what the gigantic structure looks like in polarized light. As polarized light waves have a different direction and brightness compared to unpolarized light, the new picture displays the black hole in considerably greater detail. Polarization is a characteristic of magnetic fields and the picture makes it evident that the black hole's ring is magnetized.

Following the publication of the first photograph of a black hole in 2019, scientists acquired a fresh polarized view of the black hole.

What Do Black Holes Look Like?

Black holes have three "layers": the outside and inner event horizon, and the singularity.

The event horizon of a black hole is the barrier surrounding the entrance of the black hole, beyond which light cannot escape. Once a particle reaches the event horizon, it cannot depart. Gravity is constant over the event horizon.

The inner area of a black hole, where the object's mass resides, is known as its singularity, the one point in space-time where the mass of the black hole is concentrated.

Scientists can not detect black holes the way they can see stars and other things in space. Instead, astronomers must depend on detecting the radiation black holes generate when dust and gas are pulled into the dense entities. But supermassive black holes, lurking at the heart of a galaxy, may get hidden by the heavy dust and gas surrounding them, which may mask the telltale emissions.

Sometimes, when a matter is dragged into a black hole, it ricochets off the event horizon and is thrown outward, rather than being yanked into the maw. Bright jets of material flying at near-relativistic speeds are generated. Although the black hole remains hidden, these strong jets may be spotted from considerable distances.

The EHT's photograph of a black hole in M87 (published in 2019) was an amazing endeavor, taking two years of investigation even after the photos were collected. That's because the partnership of telescopes, which spreads across numerous observatories globally, creates an astonishing quantity of data that is too vast to transport through the internet.

With time, researchers plan to scan more black holes and build up an archive of what the objects look like. The next target is presumably Sagittarius A*, which is the black hole at the heart of our own Milky Way galaxy. Sagittarius A* is fascinating because it is quieter than predicted, which may be owing to magnetic forces suppressing its activity, a 2019 research concluded. Another investigation that year found that a cold gas ring surrounds Sagittarius A*, which offers unparalleled insight into what the atmosphere surrounding a black hole looks like.

ESO's black hole anatomy graphic explains what a black hole looks like and names the major components.

Types Of Black Holes

So far, astronomers have detected three kinds of black holes: star black holes, supermassive black holes, and intermediate black holes.
Stellar black holes – tiny but dangerous
When a star burns up the rest of its fuel, the object may collapse, or fall into itself. For smaller stars (those up to around three times the sun's mass), the new core will become a neutron star or a white dwarf. But when a massive star collapses, it continues to compress and generates a stellar black hole.

Black holes generated by the collapse of individual stars are relatively tiny yet immensely dense. One of these things compresses more than three times the mass of the sun into the diameter of a city. This leads to a ridiculous amount of gravitational force tugging on items surrounding the object. Stellar black holes subsequently eat the dust and gas from their surrounding galaxies, which keeps them increasing in size.

Supermassive black holes – the origin of giants

Small black holes pervade the cosmos, while their relatives, supermassive black holes, dominate. These huge black holes are millions or even billions of times as massive as the sun yet are around the same size in diameter. Such black holes are assumed to lurk in the heart of very much every galaxy, including the Milky Way.

Scientists are not clear how such huge black holes spawn. Once these giants have formed, they acquire mass from the dust and gas surrounding them, material that is abundant at the core of galaxies, letting them expand to ever more massive sizes.
Supermassive black holes may be the product of hundreds or thousands of microscopic black holes that combine. Large gas clouds might potentially be involved, compressing together and quickly accreting mass.

A third alternative is the collapse of a stellar cluster, a collection of stars all tumbling together. Fourth, supermassive black holes might develop from vast groupings of dark matter. This is a material that we can perceive by its gravitational impact on other things; but, we do not know what dark matter is constituted of since it does not produce light and cannot be directly examined.

Intermediate black holes

Scientists long assumed that black holes existed in only tiny and big sizes, but study has shown the potential that midsize, or intermediate, black holes (IMBHs) might occur. Such things might arise when stars in a cluster clash in a chain reaction. Several of these IMBHs growing in the same location might ultimately crash together in the core of a galaxy and generate a supermassive black hole.

In 2014, scientists spotted what seemed to be an intermediate-mass black hole in the arm of a spiral galaxy. And in 2021 scientists took use of an old gamma-ray burst to identify one.

Binary black holes: double peril

In 2015, scientists using the Laser Interferometer Gravitational-Wave Observatory (LIGO) observed gravitational waves from merging star black holes.

"There is more proof of the presence of stellar-mass black holes that are bigger than 20 solar masses – these are things scientists did not know existed until

LIGO found them," David Shoemaker, the spokesman for the LIGO Scientific Collaboration (LSC), said in a statement. LIGO's findings also give information into the direction a black hole spins. As two black holes spiral around one another, they might spin in the same direction or the opposite way.

There are two hypotheses on how binary black holes arise. The first proposes that the two black holes in a binary develop at approximately the same time, from two stars that were born together and perished explosively at around the same moment. The companion stars would have had the same spin orientation as one another, therefore the two black holes left behind would as well.

Under the second hypothesis, black holes in a star cluster sink to the center of the cluster and team up. These partners would have random spin orientations relative to one another according to LIGO Scientific Collaboration. LIGO's findings of partner black holes with differing spin orientations give greater support for this formation idea.

CHAPTER 2

BLACK HOLE FACTS

If you went into a black hole, the theory has long indicated that gravity would stretch you out like spaghetti, however, your death would occur before you reached the singularity. But a 2012 research published in the journal Nature revealed that quantum processes would lead the event horizon to operate much like a wall of fire, which would instantaneously burn you to death.

Black holes do not suck. Suction is created by dragging anything into a vacuum, which the gigantic black hole surely is not. Instead, items fall into them exactly like they fall into anything that produces gravity, like the Earth.

The first object assumed to be a black hole is Cygnus X-1. Cygnus X-1 was the topic of a 1974 friendly wager between Stephen Hawking and fellow physicist Kip Thorne, with Hawking wagering that the source was not a black hole. In 1990, Hawking accepted defeat.

Miniature black holes may have developed quickly after the Big Bang. Rapidly expanding space may have crushed certain parts into small, dense black holes less massive than the sun.

If a star approaches too near a black hole, the star might be split apart.

Astronomers think that the Milky Way possesses anywhere from 10 million to

1 billion star black holes, with masses around three times that of the sun.

What Would Happen If You Fell Into A Black Hole?

The black hole; is interesting, mysterious, and terrible.
Something is unsettling about the term "black hole". It evokes emptiness, and incites sentiments of danger; it refers to something that may lure us in and entrap us. A realm where time means nothing, with mind-blowing features that humans fail to understand.
So what is a black hole? How can something that is basically "invisible nothing" be so significant and so

powerful? It's all about gravity, and the attraction of black holes, that make them so interesting.

How Are They Made?

Black holes are produced from the tiny, dense, leftover cores of dying stars. If the core's mass is more than around three times the mass of the Sun, the force of gravity overwhelms all the other forces, and the remnant collapses and becomes a black hole.

Black holes are objects with tremendous density, and the amount of mass they have means they have so much gravitational attraction that even light becomes imprisoned. Astronomers think that most spiral and elliptical galaxies feature black holes at their cores.

There are three forms of the black hole. Stellar-mass black holes are the smallest; between 1 to 100 times the mass of the Sun. They develop when the core of a big star collapses, generating a supernova (the explosion of a star).

The biggest, known as supermassive black holes, may have masses that are millions if not billions of times the mass of the Sun. It is assumed that this sort of black hole acquires its massive size through merging with other black holes, as well as by subsuming stars.

Intermediate-mass black holes are a third group that – as the name implies – sits midway between the previous two. They are still a bit of a mystery, with just a handful having been found, but they're each thought to have a mass of between 100 and 100,000 Suns. It is assumed that these are the black holes that combine to generate the supermassive variety.

Why Are They Important?

Not only can black holes explain the apparent erratic orbits of certain stars and help make sense of our galaxy, but they represent a new area of physics for scientists. Einstein's theory of general relativity6 argues that stuff warps time and space, causing what we call gravity

— and black holes are extraordinarily dense conglomerations of matter, thus their immense gravitational attraction. But from then on in – very literally – they put Einstein's hypothesis to the test.

When we look at the core of a black hole - the 'singularity' – everything becomes complex. The forces at play there are so vast that scientists can't agree on what occurs next. Einstein's general relativity predicts that when a matter is sucked into a black hole, its information is annihilated — but quantum mechanics says that cannot happen.

As a consequence, black holes are an extraordinary theoretical playground for astrophysicists and mathematicians, striving to reconcile the two ideas. From general relativity to quantum physics and string theory, black holes provide specialists with a testing ground for basic ideas that explain how the world functions.

Can We See Them?

Black holes have such a tremendous gravitational force that not even light can escape, hence they cannot be viewed directly. As a consequence, enormous radio telescopes and gravitational wave detectors are utilized instead of traditional telescopes.

In 1915, Albert Einstein proposed that as things move through space, they form waves in spacetime (a notion that merges space and time) around them, exactly like ripples flowing over the surface of a pond. Then, a century later in 2015, this was confirmed true when gravitational waves were discovered for the first time by astronomers at the Laser Interferometer Gravitational-Wave Observatory (LIGO) (LIGO). This was generated by two black holes colliding, 1.3 billion years previously.

Black holes may be identified by the impact they have on what is surrounding them - they suck in gas, dust, and stars, which get superheated and emits radiation that can then be 'seen' as a thermal picture.

In April 2019, a picture of a black hole and its shadow in the galaxy Messier 87, part of the Virgo galaxy cluster, was obtained for the first time using the Event Horizon Telescope, an array of eight ground-based radio telescopes particularly intended to capture photographs of a black hole. The picture reveals a brilliant ring surrounding a black hole 6.5 billion times more massive than the Sun, 55 million light-years from Earth. This 'halo' is the real representation of the heat put off by hot gas spinning around the event horizon — the extreme edge of the black hole – as it's being drawn in.

What Would Happen If You Fell Inside One?

So, the big question — what would happen if you went into a black hole? Well, the prognosis is not excellent, to be frank, whatever form of the black hole you selected.

If you leaped bravely into a stellar-mass black hole, your body would be subjected to a process termed 'spaghettification'. The black hole's gravitational pull would crush you from head to toe, while stretching you at the same time… therefore, spaghetti.

A supermassive black hole has a somewhat less dreadful impact, thus, assume then that you pick one of them to make your huge leap for humanity and scientific study.

Sagittarius A* (pronounced "Sagittarius A-star", and abbreviated as Sgr A*) is a supermassive black hole in the center of the Milky Way, thought to be over 44 million km wide and containing around 4.31 million solar masses.

12 It was discovered in 1974 by two astronomers, Bruce Balick and Robert L Brown, but remained unnamed until 1982.

Journeying into Sagittarius A* itself would begin once you slide beyond the event horizon, the point of no return. You would be able to see out from inside, but no one would be able to see you because any light would fall back on you. The good news is that although the gravitational pull is much stronger than smaller black holes, the stretching tidal force is less, meaning you won't be turned into spaghetti. But the bad news is you wouldn't be able to get out.

The hope of getting out lies in the theory of "white holes". Put simply, if a black hole pulls things in, then a white hole spits them out again – wherever that may be – and the two are linked by an inter-dimensional tunnel, known as a wormhole. Or, it is also hypothesized, that if you waited long enough, the black hole will transform into a white one, regardless.

This process is thought to take billions of years, but there is no reason to be disheartened. Why? Well, because of the high gravitational forces inside, time would be speeded up for you - thus everything would be over in a matter of moments. Of course, at now, this is merely a hypothesis.

If you want additional evidence of the inadvisability of swan-diving into a black hole, consider the 'tidal disruption' picked up by three Astronomers' telescopes in 2014. It was generated by a star that had gotten too near to a black hole in the heart of a galaxy, around 290 million light-years distant. It was deformed, stretched, and ripped as it was drawn into the singularity, while the remnant of the exploded star was blasted out in a 'cosmic belch'.

How Do Black Holes Sound?

In the vacuum of space, you can't hear much, but lately, it has been shown that black holes generated sounds that sound like ghostly extraterrestrial groans and wails.

The real sound, however, is out of the human hearing range at 57 octaves below middle C. The Chandra X-ray Observatory obtained data from the ripples in the Perseus cluster, visible in X-ray data, that correlated to inaudible noises.

The music originates from the Chandra telescope's X-ray data, but also contains audio interpretations of optical data from the Hubble Space Telescope and radio waves from the Atacama Large Millimeter Array in Chile. Because that data combination required more creativity than simply scaling up the pitch of a sound, it was made into beautiful music. The loudest part of the M87 music corresponds to the brightest part of the image — precisely where the black hole is.

Black hole, the dark cauldron from which nothing comes out, has been made more ghostly and ominous as new sound emerging from the cosmic object is released. The Astronomers picked up the sound from the black hole in the heart of the Perseus galaxy cluster.

A black hole is generated from the death of a star with such a powerful gravitational field that the stuff is compressed into the little region beneath it, trapping the light of the dead star. The gravity is so powerful owing to the substance being compressed into a compact space. Since no light can get out, humans can not perceive black holes. They are invisible.

While it is known that sound cannot travel in a vacuum, the galaxy cluster contains so much gas, that the Chandra observatory picked up sound, which was then amplified, and blended with other data, to hear a black hole.

Astronomers have said that a galaxy cluster has copious amounts of gas that envelop the hundreds or even thousands of galaxies within it, providing a medium for the sound waves to travel. The sound data was first captured in 2003 and it was extracted to make it audible. The sound was the consequence of pressure waves thrown out by the black hole generating ripples in the cluster's heated gas that might be translated into a note.